How to Tie a Ribbon Bow

Cross over ribbon, forming a loop.

Pinch the center of the bow together.

Wrap 2 strands of thread around the pinch several times.

Tie a knot in the thread.

Mitten Card

Warm hands, warm hearts!

This cheery greeting makes a great birthday card for anyone born in the winter season.

SIZE: 4¼" x 5½"

MATERIALS:
Cardstock (Red, White) • Mittens print paper • Lavender lightweight paper for folding • 15" White satin ¼" wide ribbon • Velvet paper ribbon for cuff • Optional Diamond Glaze • Adhesive

INSTRUCTIONS:
Card: Fold Red cardstock to make a 4¼" x 5½" card. Cut mittens paper 3⅞" x 5⅛". Adhere to card.

Iris: Cut Red cardstock 2⅞" x 4". Trace pattern and cut out. Cut Lavender paper into ¾" strips. Fold over ⅓. Follow pattern instructions. Cut White cardstock for center. Cut out Red heart. Coat heart with Diamond Glaze if desired. Adhere Iris to card.

Finish: Cut velvet ribbon 2" long and adhere to White cardstock. Trace and cut out the cuff. Place ribbon across the top. Tie a bow and adhere over ribbon, just left of center.

Cuff Pattern

Pattern A

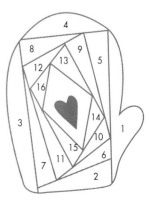

Pattern B

Halloween Scrapbook Page

by Paula Phillips

Great Tips and Ideas

Turning stickers into dimensional titles

Adhere sticker to cardboard. Trim around the sticker. Punch holes on the ends with a Crop-A-Dile or a paper piercer. Ink the edges. Lightly sand the outside edge. Thread and tie ribbon through the holes. Attach to the page with Pop Dots.

Making elements from printed papers

Printed paper makes great elements for your pages. Simply cut part of the print from the paper and attach it to the page as done here with the spider web in the top left corner.

Bat Card

I'm bats about you! Create a fun Halloween card for all your boo-tiful friends.

SIZE: 4¼" x 5½"

MATERIALS:
Orange cardstock • Black dots paper • Black lightweight paper for folding • 10" Purple satin ⅛" wide ribbon • ⅝" circle punch • 2 Black half round 3mm beads for eyes • Adhesive

INSTRUCTIONS:
Card: Fold Orange cardstock to make a 4¼" x 5½" card. Cut Dots paper 3⅞" x 5⅛". Adhere to card.
Iris: Cut Orange cardstock 3" x 4⅛". Trace pattern on diagonal and cut out. Cut Black paper into ¾" strips. Fold over ⅓. Follow pattern instructions.
Finish: Punch a ¾" circle for the head. Cut out ears and tiny bats. Adhere head, beads for eyes, ears, and tiny bats to card. Tie a ribbon bow and glue in place.

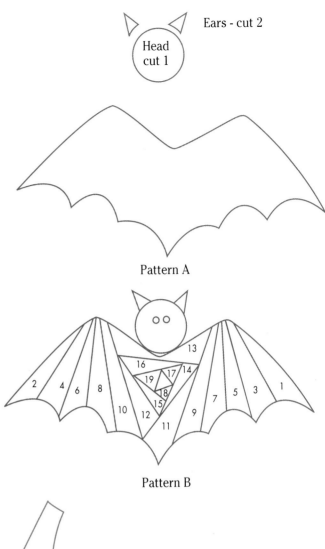

Ears - cut 2

Head cut 1

Pattern A

Pattern B

Pattern A

Leaf cut 2

Stem cut 1

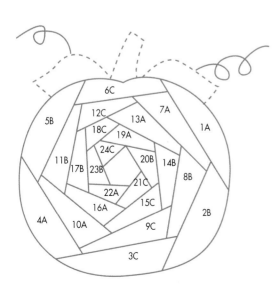

Pattern B

Pumpkin Card

Harvest time is a season of thanksgiving and sharing with family and friends. Create this great pumpkin card as a greeting or invitation.

SIZE: 4¼" x 5½"

MATERIALS:
Cardstock (Rust, Brown, White, Green) • Lightweight paper for folding (Pumpkin print, Orange plaid, Orange dot) • Decorative edge scissors • Adhesive

INSTRUCTIONS:
Card: Fold Rust cardstock to make a 4¼" x 5½" card. Cut Brown cardstock 3¾" x 4⅞". Adhere to card.
Iris: Cut White cardstock 3½" x 4⅝". Trace pattern and cut out. Cut Orange folding papers into ¾" strips. Fold over ⅓. Follow pattern instructions. Letters A use pumpkin print; B use Orange dot; C use plaid. Adhere the iris to card.
Finish: Trace leaf pattern and cut out using decorative edge scissors. Cut out stem. Cut a Green strip 1/16" x 6" for vine. Cut into 2 pieces and wrap around a toothpick to curl. Adhere leaves, stem and vines to the card.

29 again? Scrapbook Page

by Paula Phillips

Great Tips and Ideas

Customize your photo corners:

If you don't have photo corners to match your layout, it's very simple to make them yourself.

Cut a paper triangle. Stamp an image onto the triangle making sure that the image doesn't go over the edges of the paper. On the edge that will be the inside of the photo corner, trim the paper leaving a ⅛" border around the stamped image. Mount the stamped triangle onto a larger paper of a contrasting color. Trim leaving a ⅛" border on all sides. Repeat this process for the number of photo corners you will need.

Dress up plain chipboard shapes:

Choose a paper and turn it face down on the table. Place the chipboard so that the side you want covered is face down on the table on top of the paper. Trace the chipboard piece and cut out. Spread Mod Podge or a liquid adhesive onto the chipboard shape and adhere the paper. Let it dry. Use a sanding block or sandpaper to sand along the edges and give it a worn or distressed look. The more you sand, the more distressed it will appear. You can sand the top of the paper also.

Pattern A

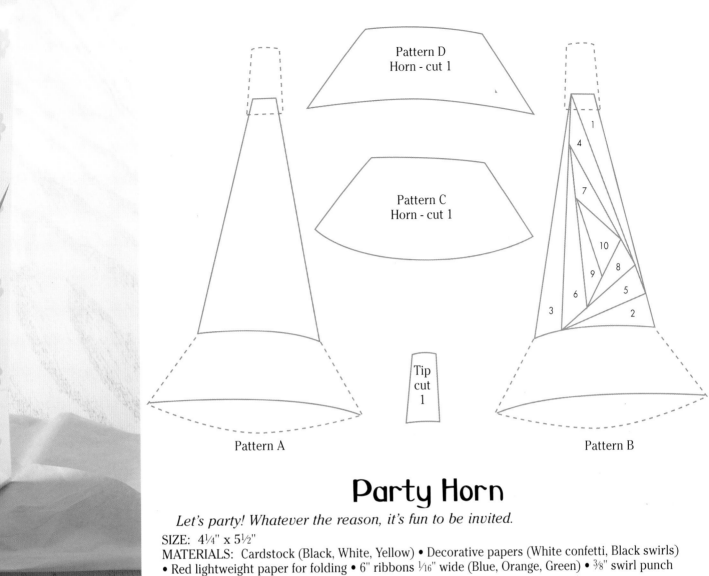

Pattern D
Horn - cut 1

Pattern C
Horn - cut 1

Tip
cut
1

Pattern A

Pattern B

Party Horn

Let's party! Whatever the reason, it's fun to be invited.

SIZE: 4¼" x 5½"

MATERIALS: Cardstock (Black, White, Yellow) • Decorative papers (White confetti, Black swirls) • Red lightweight paper for folding • 6" ribbons ¹⁄₁₆" wide (Blue, Orange, Green) • ⅜" swirl punch • Foam tape • Adhesive

INSTRUCTIONS:

Card: Fold Black cardstock to make a 4¼" x 5½" card. Cut Confetti paper 3⅞" x 5⅛". Adhere to card.

Iris: Cut White cardstock 3¼" x 4½". Trace pattern on the diagonal and cut out middle of horn. Cut Red folding papers into ¾" strips. Fold over ⅓. Follow pattern instructions. Adhere iris to card.

Finish: Cut pattern C from Black cardstock. Cut pattern D from Black swirls paper and Black cardstock. Glue D pieces together for stability. Adhere C to D with foam tape. Cut out Yellow horn mouthpiece tip. Adhere to card. Tie ribbons in a bow. Punch swirls. Adhere bow and swirls to card.

Rubber Ducky

Another birthday...you lucky Duck! Change the words and this fun card is perfect for a baby shower.

SIZE: 4¼" x 5½"

MATERIALS: Cardstock (Yellow, White, Orange) • White duck pattern paper • Yellow lightweight paper for folding • 6" Black satin ribbon (⅛" wide, ⅝" wide) • Black half round 3mm bead for eye • Adhesive

INSTRUCTIONS:

Card: Fold Yellow cardstock to make a 4¼" x 5½" card. Cut duck pattern paper mat 3¾" x 5¼". Cut a Yellow mat 3⅛" x 4". Adhere mats to card.

Iris: Cut White cardstock 2⅞" x 3¾". Trace pattern and cut out. Cut Yellow folding papers into ¾" strips. Fold over ⅓. Follow pattern instructions, beginning with A. Glue bead for eye and Orange beak in place. Adhere iris to card.

Finish: Cut a White and Yellow tag ¾" x 2¼". Adhere to card. To form a bow, make a 1" loop with ⅝" ribbon and tie with ⅛" ribbon. Hide the ⅛" ribbon tails behind the bow with glue. Adhere bow to card.

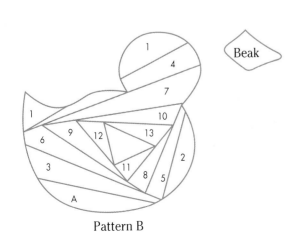

Beak

Pattern B

Coyote Card

Looking for an appropriate card for the men in your family? Try this fun Coyote. Denim paper and bandanna fabric give this a card a western flavor.

SIZE: 4¼" x 5½"

MATERIALS:

Cardstock (Red, White, Silver) • Blue dot paper • Denim lightweight paper for folding • 3" x 3" bandanna print fabric • Red thread • Adhesive

INSTRUCTIONS:

Card: Fold Red cardstock to make a 4¼" x 5½" card. Cut Blue dot paper 3⅞" x 5⅛". Adhere to card.

Iris: Cut White cardstock 3¼" x 4½". Trace pattern and cut out. Cut Denim folding papers into ¾" strips. Fold over ⅓. Follow pattern instructions in the following order: A, 1,2, B, C no fold, 3-7, D no fold, 8-14, Center. Adhere iris to card.

Finish: Cut out scarf from fabric. Treat edges with Fray Check. Let dry. Pinch fabric as indicated on pattern and wrap doubled thread around it several times. Tie a knot. Adhere to card. • Cut out foot from Denim paper and moon from Silver paper. Adhere foot and moon to card.

Mexican Hat Card

Fiesta time! Celebrate a retirement, birthday, or Cinco de Mayo with this snappy sombrero in carnival colors. Add a name to the hat brim to continue the theme, and use as table place cards.

SIZE: 4¼" x 5½"

MATERIALS:

Cardstock (Turquoise, Gold, Red, Green) • Yellow confetti print paper • Yellow pinstripe lightweight paper for folding • 3" rick rack ³⁄₁₆" wide (Red, Orange) • Punches (Swirl, Daisy, Sunburst, ⅛" circle) • Adhesive

INSTRUCTIONS:

Card: Fold Turquoise cardstock to make a 4¼" x 5½" card. Cut confetti paper 3⅞" x 5⅛". Adhere to card.

Iris: Cut Turquoise cardstock 3⅛" x 4¼". Trace pattern and cut out. Cut Gold cardstock 1" x 1⅝". Place across bottom of the cut out pattern. Cut Yellow folding papers into ¾" strips. Fold over ⅓. Follow pattern instructions. Adhere iris to card.

Finish: Cut out the hat brim from folding paper. Glue rick rack across the brim. Adhere to the card. Punch out and adhere flowers, swirls, and dots.

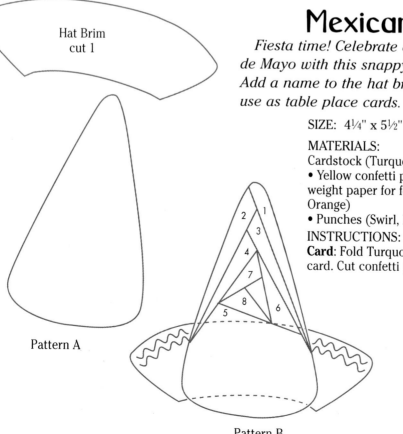

Hat Brim
cut 1

Pattern A

Pattern B

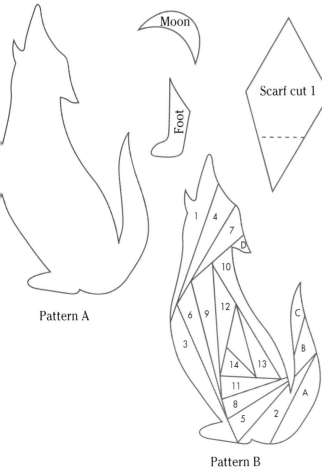

Moon

Foot

Scarf cut 1

Pattern A

1 4
7
D
10
6 9 12
3
C
B
14 13
11 A
8
5 2

Pattern B

Chili Pepper

Spice up your card collection with a Chili Pepper dressed in glossy red-hot paper.

SIZE: 4¼" x 5½"

MATERIALS:
Cardstock (Light Gray, Red, White, Green) • Red glossy lightweight paper for folding • Adhesive

INSTRUCTIONS:

Card: Fold Gray cardstock to make a 4¼" x 5½" card. Cut a Red mat 3½" x 4½" and adhere to card.

Iris: Cut White cardstock 3¼" x 4¼". Trace pattern and cut out. Cut Red glossy folding papers into ¾" strips. Fold over ⅓. Follow pattern instructions. Adhere iris to card.

Finish: Cut stem from Green cardstock. Adhere to card.

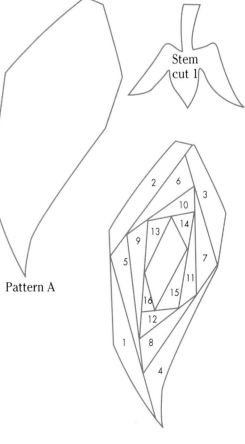

Stem cut 1

Pattern A

2 6
3
10
13 14
9
5 7
11
16 15
12
1 8
4

Pattern B

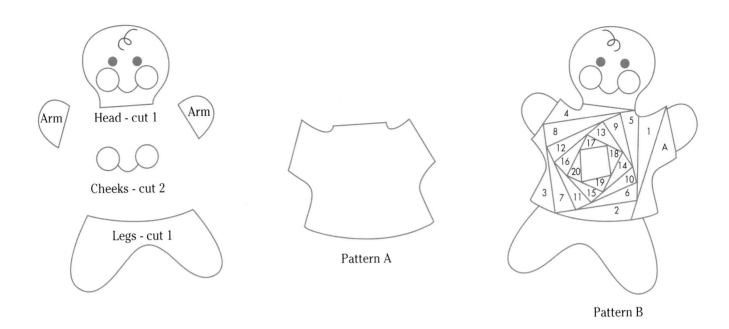

Gingerbread Boy & Girl

Kids of all ages love to get mail, especially during the holidays. Send Gingerbread greetings to all the children in the family.

SIZE: 4¼" x 5½"

MATERIALS:
Cardstock (Green, Brown, White, Red)
• Gingerbread print paper • Red glossy lightweight paper for folding • Green rick rack ³/₁₆" wide • 4" Red ribbons (⅛" wide for boy, ¼" wide for girl) • Red thread • 2 Black 3mm half round beads for eyes • ¼" circle punch • Adhesive

INSTRUCTIONS:
Card: Fold Green cardstock to make a 4¼" x 5½" card. Cut Gingerbread paper mat 4" x 5¼". Cut a Green mat 2⅝" x 3⅝". Adhere mats to card.

Iris: Cut White cardstock 2⅜" x 3⅜". Trace pattern but only cut out the shirt for iris folding. Cut Red glossy folding papers into ¾" strips. Fold over ½. Follow pattern instructions beginning with A, then numbers. Adhere iris to card.
Finish: Cut out head, arms and legs from Brown cardstock. Punch 2 Red circles for cheeks. If desired, coat Red circles with Diamond Glaze and let dry. • Cut 2 ribbons 4" long for bow. Cross ends over to make a loop. Pinch center and wrap a double piece of thread around several times. Tie a knot. Adhere parts as shown in photo.
Boy: Adhere the rick rack down the center of the shirt and add bow tie.
Girl: Adhere rick rack at neck, sleeves, and shirt bottom. Adhere bow in her hair.

BOY   GIRL

Holiday Baking Scrapbook Page

by Paula Phillips

Iris Folding motifs make fabulous embellishments on your seasonal scrapbook pages. Next time you preserve the fun of holiday baking, spice up your page with the gingerbread boy and girl.

Great Tips and Ideas

Recoloring flowers to match your page: Place a light colored flower on a protected surface and rub a stamp pad all over it until you achieve the desired color. On this page, the large flower was originally Tan.

Journaling on ribbons: When a simple phrase will do for your journaling, create a cute ribbon. Stamp the words onto the ribbon and let it dry before attaching to the page. You can also ink the edge of the ribbon with the stamp pad. This technique works best on cotton ribbons. Test a small piece to insure the ink does not rub off.

Lacing along the photo edge: Mount the photo to the page. Pierce an equal number of holes along the edge of your photo and just outside the edge. Be sure to pierce all layers. Lace the string as a shoe. Tie a knot and then a bow at the top. For wider ribbons, use a hole punch rather than a paper piercing tool.

patterns for boy and girl on page 11

Happy Holidays Scrapbook Page

by Paula Phillips

When your page needs a touch of nature, the cardinal is a favorite.

Great Tips and Ideas

Here's a page that coordinates natural elements without any clutter. The tree takes center stage and sets the theme with holiday foliage and bright color. Cardinal iris folding and mistletoe complete the page with beautiful dimensional accents.

Notice the peppermint ornaments on the tree. Continue the theme with a candy cane die cut and slide mount.

Make your page 'Pop' by mounting the mistletoe die-cuts with Pop-Dots.

Thin strips of mistletoe paper define areas of the page.

Fold a mistletoe ribbon and staple it to the title box for an attractive, eye-catching accent.

patterns for cardinal on page 14

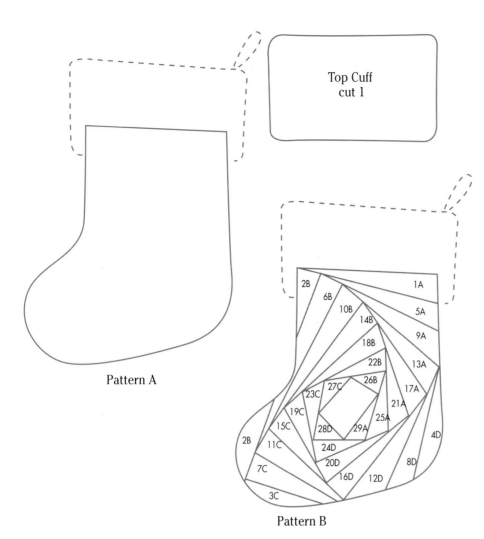

Top Cuff
cut 1

Pattern A

Pattern B

Christmas Stocking Card

The stockings were made and mailed with great care in hopes they would arrive before Santa came there. Create attractive holiday cards with this traditional motif.

SIZE: 4¼" x 5½"

MATERIALS:

Cardstock (Green, White, Red) • Lightweight paper for folding (Check, Red foil, Dots, Green foil)• White velvet paper ribbon • 2" Green satin ⅛" wide ribbon • Adhesive

INSTRUCTIONS:

Card: Fold White cardstock to make a 4¼" x 5½" card. Cut Green mat 3¾" x 5" and adhere to card.

Iris: Cut Red cardstock 3½" x 4¾". Trace pattern and cut out. Cut folding papers into ¾" strips. Fold over ⅓. Follow pattern instructions. Letter A uses Gingham paper, B uses Red foil, C uses Dots, D uses Green foil. Adhere iris to card.

Finish: Adhere White ribbon to White cardstock. Cut out stocking top from pattern. Fold Green ribbon in half and attach to stocking top. Adhere to the card.

Cardinal Card

A cheery cardinal wings his way from our house to yours bearing greetings of love and holiday joy. Change the folding papers to blue for a favorite harbinger of Spring - the Bluebird.

SIZE: 4¼" x 5½"

MATERIALS:

Cardstock (Dark Green, Black, White, Gold)• Red glossy lightweight paper for folding • 3 jingle bells ¼"• 3mm half round bead for eye • 1¼" leaf punch • Adhesive

INSTRUCTIONS:

Card: Fold Dark Green cardstock to make a 4¼" x 5½" card. Cut Black mat 3¼" x 4¼" and adhere to card.

Iris: Cut White cardstock 3" x 4". Trace pattern and cut out. Cut Red folding papers into ¾" strips. Fold over ⅓. Follow pattern instructions. Adhere iris to card.

Finish: Cut the Black beak and Gold middle. Punch 3 leaves. Adhere beak, eye, leaves, and bells to the card.

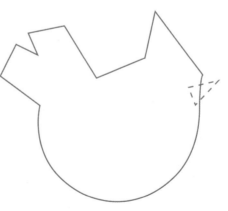

Pattern A

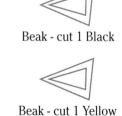

Beak - cut 1 Black

Beak - cut 1 Yellow

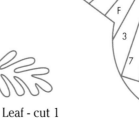

Leaf - cut 1

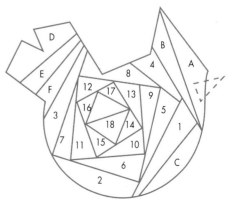

Pattern B

Star Scrapbook Page

by Paula Phillips

Great Tips and Ideas

Enhancing standard vellum titles

Using watercolor pencils, lightly color the inside edges next to the Black lines.

Using a water pen or blending pen, blend the watercolor into the center of the letter leaving the outside darker and gradually blending to little or no color in the center.

For the star, color the entire inside with the watercolor pencil and use a water or blending pen to smooth it out and give it a watercolor look. Note: To achieve a darker look on the star

Pattern A

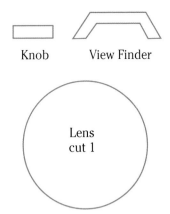

Knob   View Finder

Lens
cut 1

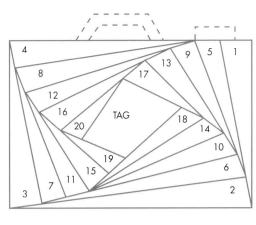

Pattern B

Camera Card

Smile! For the shutterbug in the family or a great card that will brighten someone's day, try this fun Camera card.

SIZE: 4¼" x 5½"

MATERIALS:
Cardstock (Black, White) • Papers (White camera print, Silver) • Black lightweight paper for folding • 6" Black ⅛" wide ribbon • 1½" metal rim tag • Foam tape • Adhesive

INSTRUCTIONS:
Card: Fold Black cardstock to make a 4¼" x 5½" card. Cut White camera print mat 4" x 5¼". Cut Black mat 3¼" x 4". Adhere mats.
Iris: Cut White cardstock 3" x 3¾". Trace pattern and cut out. Cut Black folding papers into ¾" strips. Fold over ⅓. Follow pattern instructions. Leave center open. Adhere iris to card.
Finish: Cut view finder and knob from Silver paper. Adhere to card. • Fold ribbon in half to make a loop. Tie the ends together in a knot. Glue to corner of camera. • Cut out photo and adhere to center of tag. Adhere to card with foam tape.

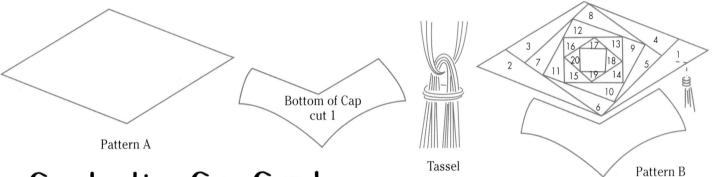

Pattern A

Bottom of Cap
cut 1

Tassel   Pattern B

Graduation Cap Card

The tassel is worth the hassle! Celebrate a worthy achievement with this wonderful card.

SIZE: 4¼" x 5½"

MATERIALS:
Cardstock (Red, Black, White) • White graduation print paper • Black lightweight paper for folding • White embroidery floss • Adhesive

INSTRUCTIONS:
Card: Fold Red cardstock to make a 4¼" x 5½" card. Cut a Black cardstock mat 3¾" x 5". Cut a White graduation print

mat 3½" x 4¾". Cut a Black mat 2⅞" x 3⅞". Adhere mats to card.
Tassel: Cut three 6" strands A; six 2½" strands B; one 1½" strand C. Fold A in half. Place B over the middle of A. Wind C around B several times. Glue to secure. Divide A into 3 parts and braid, leaving the last 1" loose. Tie a knot at the end of the braid.
Iris: Cut White cardstock 2⅝" x 3⅝". Trace pattern and cut out. Cut Black folding papers into ¾" strips. Fold over ⅓. Follow pattern instructions. Leave center open until you place the tassel in the upper right corner. Tape tassel in the back to secure. Put center piece in place. Adhere iris to card.
Finish: On front side, drape tassel and glue in place. • Cut out bottom of cap from Black folding paper. Adhere to card.

and a lighter look on the letters, use the watercolor pencils on the front for the darker look, and use them on the back of the title for a softer look.

Doodle around the edge of the title box using a fine tip pen. You can doodle stars, hearts, dots, or anything else that matches the theme of the page. Doodle dots around the inside of the star, and put some very small dots on the left inside edge of the letters to give a shadow effect.

Be sure to let the doodled vellum dry for a while before handling. Most inks do not dry instantly on vellum and will smear until completely dry.

Film strip photo frame

Cut a piece of Black paper 3¾" wide by 2½" tall. Then using the *Marvy* threaded ribbon punch, punch the top and bottom of the paper. (Optional: After punching, trim ⅛" from the top and bottom of the paper to make the punches closer to the edge.) Cut two 1⅜" squares out of the center using a craft knife. The squares should be ¼" from the sides with ¼" strip in between the squares. The squares should be ⅛" from the punched borders on the top and bottom.

If you desire more than 2 photos in the photo strip, just add 1¾" to the width of paper for each photo, follow the same instructions.

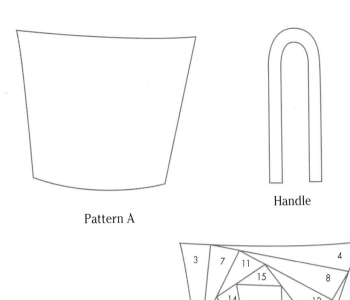

Pattern A

Handle

Easter Basket Card

Celebrate Spring with a basket brimming with brightly colored eggs or fill this basket with flowers for a unique Mother's Day or birthday card.

SIZE: 4¼" x 5½"

MATERIALS:

Cardstock (Purple, Lavender, White, Tan) • Assorted colored paper scraps for eggs • Tan check lightweight paper for folding • Easter grass • 8" Lavender ¼" ribbon • ⅝" egg punch • Foam tape • Adhesive

INSTRUCTIONS:

Card: Fold Purple cardstock to make a 4¼" x 5½" card. Cut a Lavender mat 3¾" x 5⅛" and adhere to card.

Iris: Cut White cardstock 3½" x 4⅞". Trace pattern and cut out. Cut Tan check folding papers into ¾" strips. Fold along the Dark line, about ⅓. Follow pattern instructions. Adhere iris to card.

Finish: Cut handle from Tan cardstock. • Punch eggs in several colors. Apply a double line of adhesive across the top of the basket. Roll a small amount of Easter grass between your hands. Spread grass over adhesive lines. Glue handle in place. Adhere eggs with foam tape. • Tie a bow and glue in place.

Pattern B

Bonnet Card

Whether it's an Easter bonnet or a reminder of Sunbonnet Sue, this hat makes a very lovely card.

SIZE: 4¼" x 5½"

MATERIALS:

Cardstock (Purple, White) • Lavender printed paper • Purple lightweight paper for folding • 6 lilac ⅝" silk flowers • 10" Purple sheer ½" wide ribbon • 3 pearls 3mm • Adhesive

INSTRUCTIONS:

Card: Fold Purple cardstock to make a 4¼" x 5½" card. Cut a Lavender mat 3¾" x 5" and adhere to card.

Iris: Cut White cardstock 3¼" x 4½". Trace pattern and cut out only top of hat. Cut Purple folding papers into ¾" strips. Fold over ⅓. Follow the pattern instructions. Adhere the iris to card.

Finish: Cut brim from lightweight Purple paper. If desired, cut on broken line and glue together. Adhere to card. • Separate lilac into 6 blossoms. Glue a pearl in the center of 3 blossoms and adhere to the card. • Tie a bow and adhere to hat.

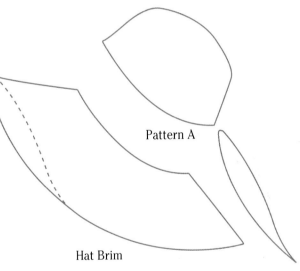

Pattern A

Hat Brim

Hat Brim Trim

Spring Scrapbook Page

by Paula Phillips

Great Tips and Ideas:

Add sizzle to your stamped images.

On the scrapbook page at left, vines and swirls were stamped. Then, Stickles or glitter glue was added in dots over the berries on the vines and on various parts of the swirl stamps. To tie the stamps and stickers together, Stickles or glitter glue was also added to parts of the stickers.

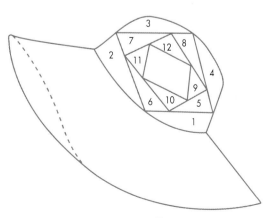

Pattern B

Flip Flop Card

The lazy days of summer are best spent in flip flops. This card is perfect when you need a relaxed, fun theme.

SIZE: 4¼" x 5½"

MATERIALS:
Cardstock (Green, White) • Yellow flip flop printed paper • Yellow lightweight paper for folding • Yellow ¼" flocked circle for daisy center • Daisy flower punch • Adhesive

INSTRUCTIONS:

Card: Fold Green cardstock to make a 4¼" x 5½" card. Cut a Yellow print mat 3⅞" x 5⅛" and adhere to card.

Iris: Cut White cardstock 3" x 4⅛". Trace pattern on diagonal and cut out. Cut Yellow folding papers into ¾" strips. Fold over ⅓. Follow pattern instructions. Adhere iris to card.

Finish: Punch 2 daisy flowers and glue together. Adhere flocked center. Cut sole and strap from Green cardstock. Adhere sole, strap, and flowers to card.

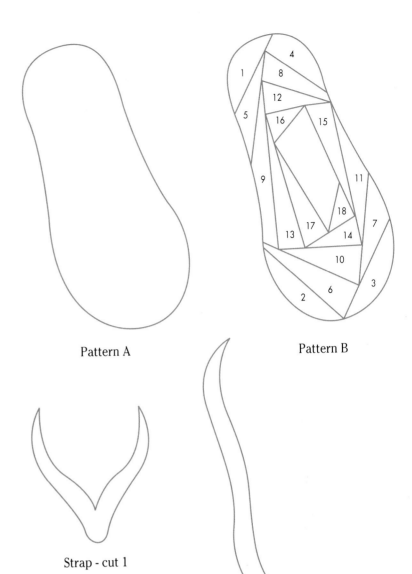

Pattern A

Pattern B

Strap - cut 1

Sole - cut 1

Pattern A

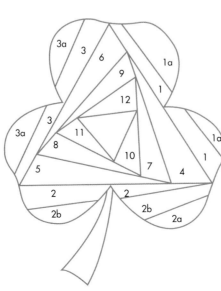

Pattern B

Shamrock Card

You won't need the luck of the Irish to complete this attractive shamrock card.

SIZE: 4¼" x 5½"

MATERIALS:
Cardstock (Green, White) • Green dot lightweight paper for folding • 10" Green satin ¼" wide ribbon • Adhesive

INSTRUCTIONS:

Card: Fold Green cardstock to make a 4¼" x 5½" card.

Iris: Cut White cardstock 3½" x 4½". Trace pattern and cut out shamrock center. Cut Green folding papers into ¾" strips. Fold over ⅓. Follow pattern instructions beginning with 1a-2a-2b-3a, then numbers.

Finish: Cut the stem from lightweight paper and adhere in place. • Cut 2 ribbons 2½" and adhere to corners of White cardstock. Use the 5" ribbon to tie a bow. Adhere over the ribbon in the upper corner. Adhere Iris to card.

Moose Card

Perfect for the nature lover, this moose card combines neutral tones that appeal so much to the men in the family.

SIZE: 4¼" x 5½"

MATERIALS:
Cardstock (Brown, Cream) • Brown check printed paper • Dark Brown lightweight paper for folding • 6" Brown ⅛" wide satin ribbon • Oak leaf ¾" punch • Adhesive

INSTRUCTIONS:

Card: Fold Brown cardstock to make a 4¼" x 5½" card. Cut a Brown check mat 3¾" x 3¾" and adhere to card.

Iris: Cut Cream cardstock 3" x 4⅛". Trace pattern and cut out. Cut Brown folding papers into ¾" strips. Fold over ⅓. Follow pattern instructions. Adhere iris to card.

Finish: Punch 5 Cream leaves and adhere to card. Tie ribbon in a knot and glue in place. To secure the cardstock, place a small dot of glue under the Cream areas indicated by dots.

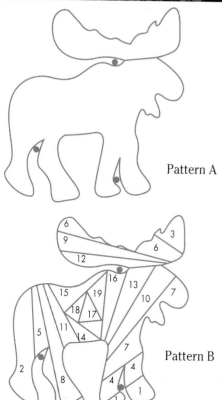

Pattern A

Pattern B

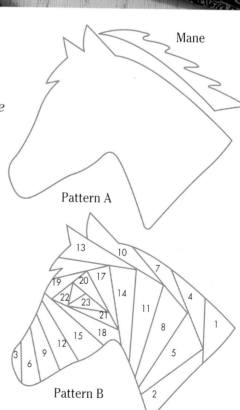

Mane

Pattern A

Pattern B

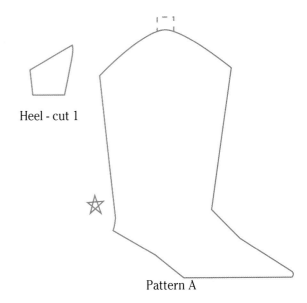

Heel - cut 1

Pattern A

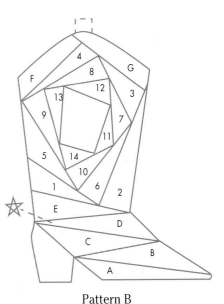

Pattern B

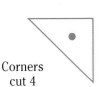

Corners
cut 4

Horse Card

Capture the unbridled spirit of the wild mustang on a beautiful card that celebrates our love of horses.

SIZE: 4¼" x 5½"

MATERIALS:

Cardstock (Brown, Cream, Black) • Gray horseshoe print paper • Brown lightweight paper for folding • 4 Gold minibrads • Adhesive

INSTRUCTIONS:

Card: Fold Brown cardstock to make a 4¼" x 5½" card. Cut a Horseshoe paper mat 4" x 5¼" and adhere to card.

Iris: Cut Cream cardstock 3¼" x 4⅛". Trace pattern and cut out. Cut Brown folding papers into ¾" strips. Fold over ⅓. Follow pattern instructions. The center piece is Black cardstock.

Finish: Cut 4 corner triangles from Brown cardstock and glue in place. Attach a brad to each corner. Adhere iris to card. Cut out mane from Brown lightweight paper and glue in place. • If desired, print "Howdy!" on a scrap of Cream cardstock and adhere to the back of the card with a cut out horseshoe from the printed paper.

Cowboy Boot

It's Rodeo Time! Nothing symbolizes the legends of the west or captures the imagination like cowboys and their famous boots.

SIZE: 4¼" x 5½"

MATERIALS:

Cardstock (Rust, Tan) • Papers (Tan stripe for heel, Blue cowboy print for mat)• Brown lightweight paper for folding • ½" Silver chain sticker for spur • ¼" Silver star • Adhesive

INSTRUCTIONS:

Card: Fold Rust cardstock to make a 4¼" x 5½" card. Cut a Cowboy print mat 4" x 5¼" and a Rust mat 3" x 4¼". Adhere mats to card.

Iris: Cut the Tan cardstock 2¾" x 3⅞". Trace iris pattern and cut out. Cut Brown folding papers into ¾" strips. Fold over ⅓. Follow pattern instructions beginning with letters A-G, then numbers. Adhere iris to the card.

Finish: Cut boot heel from Tan stripe paper. Adhere heel, Silver chain sticker, and star to card.

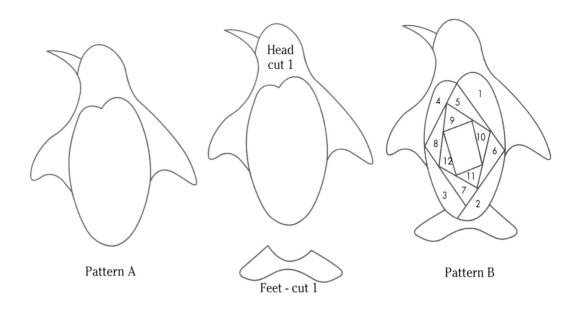

Pattern A

Head
cut 1

Feet - cut 1

Pattern B

Penguin Card

Snowy greetings! This happy penguin is right at home on this winter landscape.

SIZE: 4¼" x 5½"

MATERIALS:

Cardstock (White, Blue, Black, Orange) • Blue stripe paper • White glossy lightweight paper for folding • White sequin • White plastic ⅜" snowflake • Adhesive

INSTRUCTIONS:

Card: Fold White cardstock to make a 4¼" x 5½" card. Cut a Blue cardstock mat 3⅛" x 4½" and adhere to card.

Iris: Cut a Stripe mat 2⅞" x 4¼". Tear strips across top of White cardstock 1¼" x 2⅞" and ¾" x 2⅞". Adhere strips in layers at the bottom. Trace pattern 1" from the snowy bottom and cut out center only. Cut White folding papers into ¾" strips. Fold over ⅓. Follow pattern instructions. Adhere iris to card.

Finish: Cut penguin body and feet from Black cardstock. Cut out Orange beak. Adhere body, feet, beak, sequin, and snowflake to card.

Snow Scrapbook Page

by Paula Phillips

Great Tips and Ideas:

Add your own sparkle:

Make your pages shine by adding Stickles or glitter glue to your purchased elements. On this page, the glitter on the snowflakes adds interest. Use your finger to spread glitter into the grooves. This technique can be done on buttons and brads as well.

Use your chipboard letters as stencils:

What do you do if you need a title, and you have the perfect chipboard letters, but they're not the right color? Use the chipboard letters as stencils and make customized letters from your favorite papers.

Turn the paper face down on the table. Place the chipboard letters face down on the paper. The letters will appear to be backwards, and that is ok. You want them this way so that when you cut them out, they will be in the correct direction on the front of the paper. Trace around the letters. Cut out the letters and adhere them to page. Voila! You now have perfectly matched letters for a title.

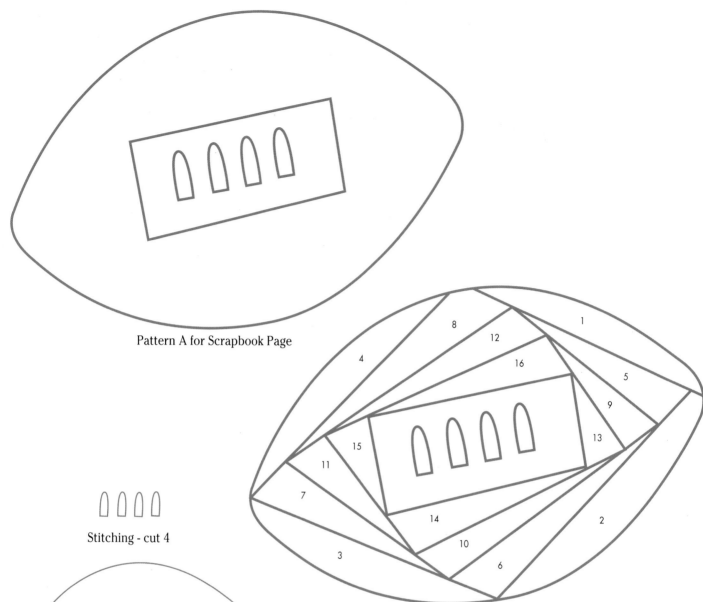

Pattern A for Scrapbook Page

Stitching - cut 4

Pattern A

Pattern B for Scrapbook Page

Football Card

Share the excitement of Homecoming season and the rivalry of your favorite teams with a card that scores a touchdown every time.

SIZE: 4¼" x 5½"

MATERIALS:

Cardstock (Green, Tan, White)• Football words paper • Brown lightweight paper for folding • Adhesive

INSTRUCTIONS:

Card: Fold Green cardstock to make a 4¼" x 5½" card.

Iris: Cut a Words mat 4" x 5¼". Trace pattern and cut out. Cut folding papers into ¾" strips. Cut a 3" piece for the center but do not fold. Fold remaining strips over ⅓. Follow pattern instructions. Adhere iris to card.

Finish: Cut a 1¼" White strip ¹⁄₁₆" wide. Cut into 4 pieces ⁵⁄₁₆" long. Round one end of each strip with scissors and adhere to center piece of football for stitching. • Cut Tan cardstock goal posts ⅛" wide: two 3¼", one 4¼". Adhere to card.

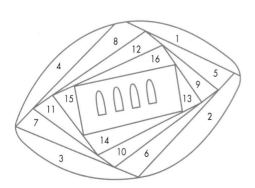

Pattern B

Football Scrapbook Page

by Paula Phillips

Team spirit fills this page with the colors of America's favorite sport.

Great Tips and Ideas

Make the large Iris Folding football by cutting 1" strips of Brown decorative paper (not cardstock, it is too thick). Fold each strip in half then position and tape as usual. Cut four 3/16" x 5/8" strips of White cardstock. Adhere these in the center of the football.

Mark the playing field with quarter inch wide White cardstock stripes. Use die-cut yard numbers or make your own- just computer print the numbers on White cardstock with Brown ink and cut them out.

The die-cut "Touchdown" title cleverly represents the goal posts and the football iris fold is perfect for this page.

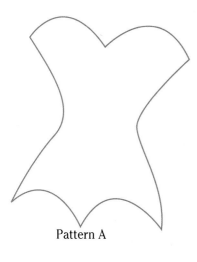

Pattern A

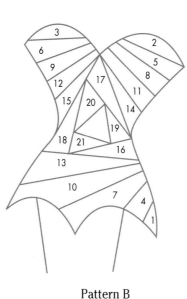

Pattern B

Corset Card

Of Corset's your Birthday! Create a charming card with a sense of humor.

SIZE: 4¼" x 5½"

MATERIALS:
Cardstock (Light Pink, Pink, White) • Pink Lace lightweight paper for folding • 5" White ⅛" wide satin ribbon • ½" lace flower • ⅜" Pink satin rose • 8" White loop fringe ⅛" wide ribbon • Black pen • Adhesive

INSTRUCTIONS:
Card: Fold Pink cardstock to make a 4¼" x 5½" card. Cut a Light Pink mat 3½" x 4¼" and adhere to card.
Iris: Cut White cardstock 3¼" x 4". Trace pattern and cut out. Cut folding papers into ¾" strips. Fold over ⅓. Follow pattern instructions. Adhere iris to card.
Finish: Cut a White cardstock title mat ⅞" x 2". Print "of 'Corset's your Birthday!" and adhere to card. • Cut 2 strips of satin ribbon and adhere at bottom of corset. Glue loop fringe ribbon around top and bottom of corset. Adhere the lace flower and Pink rose.

Asian Fan Card

Elegant for any occasion, the Asian Fan makes a lovely 'thank you' or 'thinking of you' card.

SIZE: 4¼" x 5½"

MATERIALS:
Cardstock (Blue, Gold glossy, White, Black, Black glossy) • Lightweight papers for folding (Gold, Blue Asian print) • 20" Gold 1/16" elastic • *Stamp Craft* Asian stamps (Happiness, Long Life) • Black ink • Diamond Glaze • Adhesive

INSTRUCTIONS:
Card: Fold Blue cardstock to make a 4¼" x 5½" card. Cut a glossy Gold mat 3¼" x 4½" and adhere to card.
Iris: Cut White cardstock 3" x 4¼". Trace pattern and cut out. Cut folding papers into ¾" strips. Fold over ⅓. Follow pattern instructions. Even numbers use Gold, odd numbers use the Blue Asian print. Adhere iris to card.
Finish: Stamp Happiness symbol on card.
• Stamp Long Life symbol on White cardstock and cut out. Cut a Black glossy mat ⅛" larger than the stamp. Adhere to card. • Cut out handle from Black cardstock. Coat handle with Diamond Glaze. Let dry. Adhere to card. • Tie Gold elastic around the fold of the card.

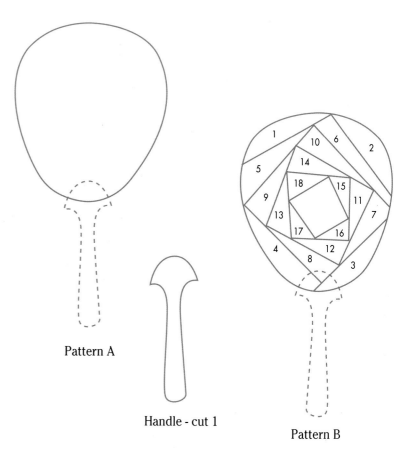

Pattern A

Handle - cut 1

Pattern B

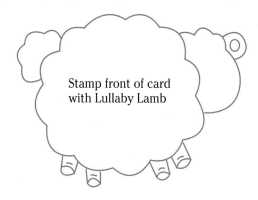

Stamp front of card
with Lullaby Lamb

Pattern A

The lamb is a
Stampabilities Lullaby
Lamb stamp #GR1081

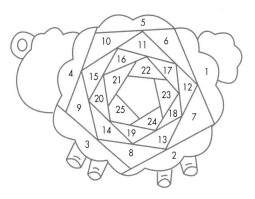

Pattern B

Lamb Card

Count your blessings as well as sheep, and know that you can always count on me. When you need to send a comforting message, this card is a warm and fluffy choice. Just remember, Ewe mean everything to me.

SIZE: 4¼" x 5½"

MATERIALS:
Cardstock (Gray, White, Black) • Pearlescent White lightweight paper for folding
• *Stampabilities* Lullaby Lamb stamp • Black ink • Colored pencils • Colored chalk
• Foam tape • Adhesive

INSTRUCTIONS:
Card: Fold Gray cardstock to make a 4¼" x 5½" card. Cut a Black mat 3⅛" x 4¼" and adhere to card.
Iris: Cut White cardstock 2⅞" x 4". Stamp lamb on front side of card and cut out middle. Turn over and place on Pattern B. Stamp extra lamb head and cut out. Cut folding papers into ¾" strips. Fold over ⅓. Follow pattern instructions. Adhere iris to the card.
Finish: Shade lamb and head with colored pencils. Use Black for the middle of ears and bottom of feet. Use Gray for legs, ears, and portions of the tail and feet. Apply Pink chalk to the cheeks and Green chalk for the grass. Attach the head with foam tape.

"Aren't Ewe Cute" Scrapbook Page

by Paula Phillips

Great Tips and Ideas:

Doodle die cuts to make them pop.

After die cutting letters, doodle around the edges with a contrasting color to add dimension. When doodling, don't worry about the lines being perfectly straight. Just draw along the inside edge of the letter and stop every so often. Make a few dots or smaller lines, then draw along the inside edge again, then doodle dots again. Repeat until you have gone all the way around the letter.

To maintain continuity on your page, pull the doodling onto other page elements. On this page, the paper strip at the bottom of the page and the frame on the top photo were doodled like the lettering. You can even doodle on photos in the same fashion to give them a framed appearance as done on the bottom two photos.

3D Buttons and Ribbons:

Add dimension and interest by using different sizes of Pop Dots or dimensional adhesives. The photo on page 31; different size and height dimensional dots were used to adhere the buttons to the page. This allows them to slightly overlap.

On the bottom of the page, dimensional dots were used, and then ribbon was tied around the dimensional dots. This not only helps to hide the dimensional dots on smaller elements, but also adds additional depth.

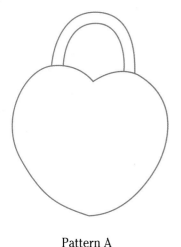

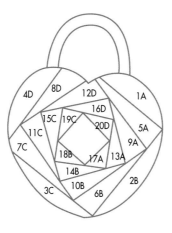

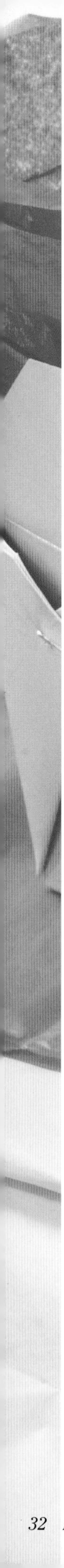

Pattern A

Pattern B

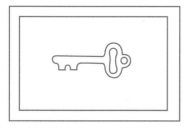

Lock and Key Card

You hold the key to my heart. Make this beautifully unusual card for Valentine's Day, an anniversary, or just to say "I love you."

SIZE: 4¼" x 5½"

MATERIALS:

Cardstock (Red, White, Black) • Lightweight papers for folding (Black, Red mini hearts, Hearts on Black, Red with White hearts) • ½" square Gold heart • ¾" Gold key • 20" Red ⅛" wide satin ribbon • Adhesive

INSTRUCTIONS:

Card: Fold Red cardstock to make a 4¼" x 5½" card. Cut a Black mat 3⅜" x 3⅜" and adhere to card.

Iris: Cut White cardstock 3" x 3". Trace and cut out heart. Cut folding papers into ¾" strips. Use Red with White hearts for A, Mini Red hearts for B, Black for C, and Hearts on Black for D. Fold over ⅓. Follow pattern instructions. Adhere iris to the card.

Finish: Cut handle from Black cardstock and adhere to card. Mount metal heart on Red cardstock and adhere to center. • Cut a Black mat 1⅛" x 2" and a White mat ¾" x 1⅛". Layer the White mat on the Black, centering the metal key. Adhere to the back of the card. • Tie ribbon around the fold.

Dressform Card

This Dressform card is just the right size for any seamstress or fabric artist in your circle of family and friends.

SIZE: 4¼" x 5½"

MATERIALS:

Cardstock (Black, White) • Red dressform print paper • Tan lightweight paper for folding • 3 Black ¼" buttons • 6" Black 20 gauge wire • 4" ribbon (Red ⅛" wide satin, Red check ¼" wide) • ⅜" Red rose • Round-nose pliers • Adhesive

INSTRUCTIONS:

Card: Fold Black cardstock to make a 4¼" x 5½" card. Cut a Red paper mat 4" x 5¼" and adhere to the card.

Iris: Cut White cardstock 2⅝" x 5". Trace pattern and cut out. Cut folding papers into ¾" strips. Fold over ⅓. Follow pattern instructions. Adhere the iris to card.

Finish: Fold wire in half and twist ¾" from the fold. Bend and curl wire ends into shape with pliers. Adhere to card. • Fold ribbons and glue in place with rose on top. Adhere buttons to card.

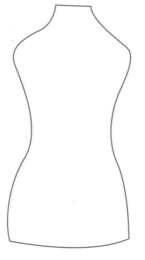

Pattern A

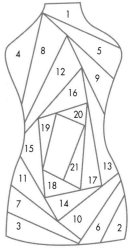

Pattern B